D0906111

PROTECTING EARTH'S
RAIN
FORESTS

ANNE WELSBACHER

LERNER PUBLICATIONS COMPANY · MINNEAPOLIS

The text of this book is printed on Lustro Offset Environmental paper, which is made with **30 percent recycled post-consumer waste fibers**. Using paper with post-consumer waste fibers helps to protect endangered forests, conserve mature trees, keep used paper out of landfills, save energy in the manufacturing process, and reduce greenhouse gas emissions. The remaining fiber comes from forestlands that are managed in a socially and environmentally responsible way, as certified by independent organizations. Also, the mills that manufactured this paper purchased certified renewable energy, such as solar or wind energy, to cover its production.

Text copyright © 2009 by Anne Welsbacher

Lerner Publications Company
A division of Lerner Publishing Group, Inc.
241 First Avenue North
Minneapolis, MN 55401 U.S.A.

Website address: www.lernerbooks.com

Library of Congress Cataloging-in-Publication Data

Welsbacher, Anne, 1955–
    Protecting Earth's rain forests / by Anne Welsbacher.
        p.   cm. — (Saving our living Earth)
    Includes bibliographical references and index.
    ISBN 978-0-8225-7562-7 (lib. bdg. : alk. paper)
    I. Rain forest ecology—Juvenile literature. 2. Rain forest—Juvenile literature. I. Title.
QH541.5.R27W44 2009
577.34—dc22   2007038859

Manufactured in the United States of America
1 2 3 4 5 6 — DP — 14 13 12 11 10 09

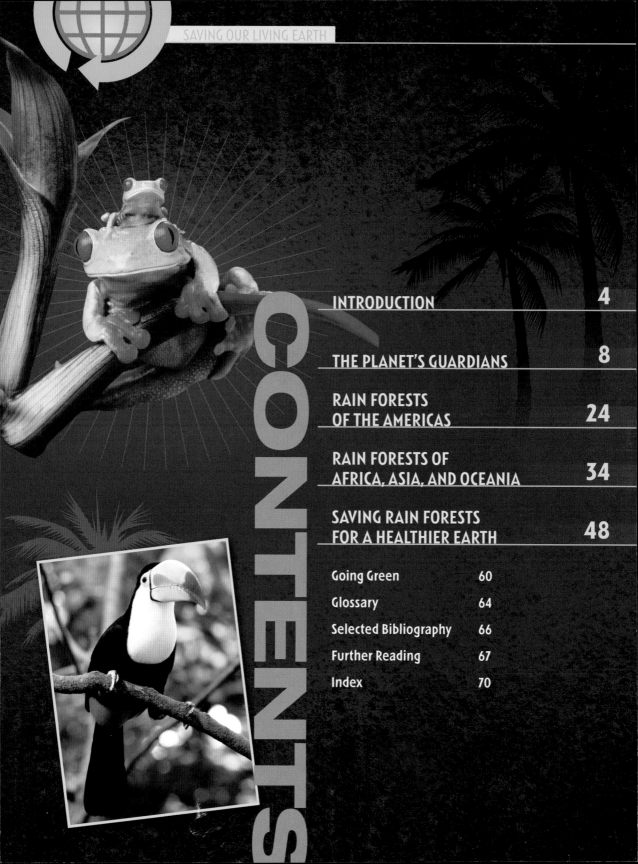

CONTENTS

INTRODUCTION

Rain forests are among the world's oldest and most important ecosystems. (An ecosystem is a community of living things that depend on one another and their shared environment.) Made up of trees that grow 100 feet (30 meters) or taller, rain forests provide homes for half the world's plants and animals. Rain forests house an amazing variety of creatures, from brilliant birds to odd insects, from stinky flowers to poisonous mushrooms, from tiny bats to giant elephants. Thousands of rain forest species live nowhere else on Earth.

Rain forests are home to thousands of humans too. And these forests are

Left: Rafflesia, the world's largest flowering plant, grows in the rain forests of Southeast Asia. *Right:* Rain forests around the globe, such as this one in Malaysia, are home to thousands of plant and animal species. *Facing page:* Many rain forest animals, such as these forest elephants, are in danger of losing their homes if rain forests disappear.

important to millions more people who don't live in them. They provide food and water for much of the world. They produce many plants that people use to make medicines. They also help control Earth's climate, prevent flooding, and hold soil in place.

Some scientists fear that by the mid-twenty-first century, rain forests might disappear completely.

Earth relies on its rain forests to keep the whole planet healthy. But all over the world, the rain forests are shrinking. Rain forests once covered about 14 percent of Earth's surface. Today they extend over only about 6 percent of our planet. People have burned or cut down more than half of the original rain forests. Some scientists fear that by the mid-twenty-first century, rain forests might disappear completely.

When a rain forest shrinks, it seriously harms the entire local area and all who live there. Thousands of people and hundreds of thousands of plant and animal species lose their homes.

This mountain on the island of Papua New Guinea, near Australia, was once covered with rain forest.

Clearing trees also changes the land. Forest plants and soil soak up rain and release it slowly. With less forest to absorb heavy rain, water tends to rush downhill. Streams and rivers overflow, flooding villages and fields.

The loss of rain forests also creates problems farther away. In fact, it creates problems worldwide. Rain forests play an important role in managing Earth's atmosphere and climate.

Plants use a process called photosynthesis to make their own food. Inside plants, sunlight powers a series of chemical reactions. These reactions change water and carbon dioxide (a gas in Earth's air) into sugar. This sugar gives plants all the energy they need to live and grow.

Because rain forests contain so many plants, they absorb large amounts of carbon dioxide from the air. When forests flourish, they store a lot of carbon. The gases in Earth's atmosphere stay in balance.

When people destroy rain forests, the forests release large amounts of carbon dioxide into the air. Carbon dioxide in the atmosphere acts like greenhouse windows. It lets in the sun's light and traps its heat near the ground. Scientists call this the greenhouse effect. They call carbon dioxide a greenhouse gas.

The greenhouse effect is slowly but steadily warming up our planet and

Hurricane Frances hits a Florida beach in September 2004. Stronger, more frequent storms may be linked with global warming. Destruction of the world's rain forests contributes to the problem of global warming.

changing its climate. Global warming and climate change cause many problems around the world. For example, warmer weather is melting the ice around the North Pole and South Pole. Melting polar ice endangers animals. It raises sea levels, which causes flooding in coastal areas. Global warming is also changing local weather patterns. In some areas, the changing weather leads to more wildfires and droughts. In other areas, it leads to stronger storms, heavier rains, and more flooding.

Scientists, world leaders, and ordinary people concerned about the health of our planet are working to slow global warming and climate change. Slowing or stopping rain forest loss is an important part of this work. How people act in the next decade could decide the future of the world's rain forests—and of Earth itself. In this book, you'll find out more about our rain forests and how people—including you—can protect the remaining rain forests.

CHAPTER ONE

THE PLANET'S GUARDIANS

Rain forests exist in many forms all over the world. They provide homes for thousands of kinds of plants and animals. All these living things depend on one another and a healthy environment. And healthy rain forests help keep our planet healthy. But what exactly makes for a healthy rain forest? In this chapter, you'll learn what types of rain forests exist on Earth and where they're found. You'll discover what lives in them and how rain forests function.

TYPES OF RAIN FORESTS

Scientists divide Earth's rain forests into two main types: tropical rain forests and temperate rain forests. Tropical rain forests get 80 to 400 inches (203 to 1,016 centimeters) of rain per year. Temperatures range between 72° and 93°F (22° and 34°C). Tropical rain forests grow on mountains and lowlands near the equator. They're found in South and Central America, West Africa, southern India, Southeast Asia, and in Oceania, an area that includes Australia and the Pacific islands.

Healthy rain forests help keep our planet healthy.

Background image: Visitors to La Selva Biological Station in Costa Rica can hike through its dense tropical rain forest. *Below:* Colorful keel-billed toucans live in rain forests from southern Mexico to Venezuela and Colombia.

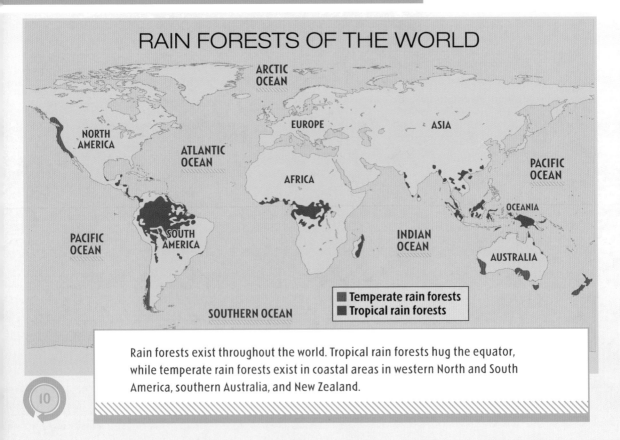

RAIN FORESTS OF THE WORLD

ARCTIC OCEAN

EUROPE

ASIA

NORTH AMERICA

ATLANTIC OCEAN

PACIFIC OCEAN

AFRICA

OCEANIA

PACIFIC OCEAN

SOUTH AMERICA

INDIAN OCEAN

AUSTRALIA

SOUTHERN OCEAN

■ Temperate rain forests
■ Tropical rain forests

Rain forests exist throughout the world. Tropical rain forests hug the equator, while temperate rain forests exist in coastal areas in western North and South America, southern Australia, and New Zealand.

Two-thirds of tropical rain forests are wet equatorial rain forests. These are rain forests found along the equator in the Amazon River lowlands in South America, the Congo River basin in Africa, and in Southeast Asia in the countries of Indonesia and Papua New Guinea. This type of rain forest contains the greatest variety of species. It has hot, rainy weather year-round.

Tropical moist forests make up the remaining one-third of tropical rain forests. These forests lie farther from the equator, where sunlight strength and day length change through the year to create seasons. During the cooler, drier season, many trees lose leaves. This lets more sunlight enter, allowing more growth on the lower levels of tropical moist forests. Tropical moist rain forests are found in parts of South America and the Caribbean, in West Africa, and in southern Asia in Thailand, Myanmar, Vietnam, and Sri Lanka.

The second main type of rain forest is the temperate rain forest. Temperate rain forests receive less rain than tropical ones: 50 to 120 inches (127 to 309 cm) per year. Most temperate rain forests grow near coasts and are called coastal temperate rain forests. They're found in western North and South America, southern Australia, and New Zealand. Like tropical moist forests, temperate rain forests have seasons.

Very few temperate rain forests remain on Earth. Although this book discusses some temperate forests, it focuses on tropical ones. On the following pages, the term *rain forest* means "tropical rain forest" unless the word *temperate* appears with it.

This temperate rain forest is located in Australia.

LAYERS OF THE RAIN FOREST

EMERGENT LAYER

CANOPY

UNDERSTORY

FOREST
FLOOR

LAYERS OF THE RAIN FOREST

A rain forest grows in layers. From top to bottom, the four main layers of a rain forest are the emergent layer, the canopy, the understory, and the forest floor.

The emergent layer is the highest and consists of very tall trees that emerge, or rise, high above most of the other treetops. These towering trees reach 165 to 213 feet (50 to 65 m) tall. Their branches stretch more than 100 feet (30 m) wide

The canopy lies below the emergent trees. The upper canopy may be 100 to 130 feet (30 to 40 m) above the ground. The lower canopy is 75 to 100 feet (23 to 30 m) high. The canopy forms a dense ceiling of leaves and tangled tree branches. It contains more than 70 percent of a rain forest's plant and animal life.

Epiphytes cover many canopy trees. Epiphytes are plants that live on other plants. They get food and water from air and rain. Epiphytes help the trees they live on. When they die and decay, their host plants absorb their nutrients.

Facing page: Scientists divide the rain forest into different layers. Epiphytes, such as ferns and bromeliads *(right),* can live only when supported by other plants. They grow mostly in the rain forest canopy.

Thick, strong vines crisscross the canopy of this tropical rain forest in Costa Rica.

14

Lianas (vines) grow up into the canopy from woody shrubs on the forest floor. They twist around tree trunks and branches, growing toward the sunlight and spreading from tree to tree. In some forests, their leaves make up 40 percent of the canopy leaves. Lianas can grow as tall and thick as trees. Some lianas strangle trees with their size and weight. But even this benefits the forest. A dead tree provides nutrients for other organisms (living things). Lianas also take in carbon dioxide from dying trees, delaying its return to the atmosphere.

JUNGLE VINES

The biggest lianas might grow 3,000 feet (914 m) long. They twine around trees. If they were to grow straight up, they would be twice as tall as the Empire State Building!

The understory is the shady area between the canopy and the ground. It exists about 5 feet (1.5 m) to 50 feet (15 m) off the forest floor. It includes many levels of leaves and branches. The lowest level—5 to 20 feet (1.5 to 6 m) above the floor—is the shrub layer. This layer consists of bushes and tree saplings.

The bottom layer of a rain forest is the forest floor. It includes the 5 feet (1.5 m) from the ground to the bottom of the understory. Few plants grow within this layer because almost no sunlight reaches this part of the rain forest. Also, most rain forests have poor soil. (Their soil is low in mineral nutrients that plants need.) When plants die and decay, they release mineral nutrients. Surviving rain forest plants absorb these nutrients very quickly, before they make their way into the soil.

THE RAIN FOREST CLIMATE

True to their name, rain forests get lots and lots of rain. What happens to all that water? When rain falls, the canopy's large leaves trap most of the water. The rest of it trickles slowly down to the soil. There a maze of roots sucks up the water to feed shrubs, vines, trees, and other plants. Because so little rain reaches the ground and because the tangled roots hold the soil in place, heavy rain doesn't erode, or wear away, the soil.

Rain forests return water to the atmosphere through a process called transpiration. During photosynthesis, tiny pores in plants open to take in carbon dioxide. At the same time, the pores release water vapor. This moisture creates more rain clouds, which eventually drop the water back on the forest as rain.

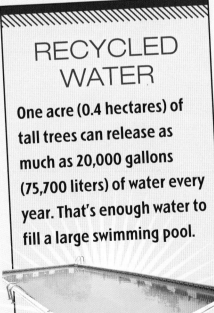

RECYCLED WATER

One acre (0.4 hectares) of tall trees can release as much as 20,000 gallons (75,700 liters) of water every year. That's enough water to fill a large swimming pool.

In this way, rain forests recycle most of their water again and again. The Amazon rain forest, for example, recycles 50 to 80 percent of its water.

The wet, warm weather in rain forests enables them to be productive and biodiverse. An ecosystem that's productive makes a lot of food for its members. A place that's biodiverse is home to many different types of living things.

Most tropical rain forests are very biodiverse. One forest can contain hundreds of species of trees alone. In addition, it can contain thousands of other plant species, animal species, and other kinds of organisms.

Because rain forests contain so many plants, in the process of photosynthesis they absorb and store a lot of carbon dioxide. When rain forest plants die, they release carbon dioxide back into the air. But in healthy rain forests, this happens slowly. The surviving plants take in the newly released carbon dioxide before it collects in the atmosphere.

16

One rain forest can contain hundreds of species of trees alone.

LIFE IN THE RAIN FORESTS

Rain forest plants and animals help one another live, grow, and reproduce. In doing so, they help the rain forest as a whole stay healthy.

For example, rain forest trees reproduce by dropping seeds to the ground. The seeds grow into new trees. Some seeds are enclosed in fruits, nuts, or other foods. These foods attract hungry animals.

When an animal eats such a food, the hard seed passes unharmed through the animal's body. By the time the seed exits in the animal's droppings, the animal

A mustached monkey eats a fruit in the jungle of Gabon, in West Africa. Animals that rely on rain forest plants often support the plants. Their droppings distribute plant seeds.

has usually moved to a different place. In this way, the animal gives the seed a better chance of growing. The animal takes the seed away from the shade of its huge parent and drops it in a new place, along with manure for fertilizer.

Animals also play an important role in pollination. Pollination is a process that enables plants to make seeds. (Most plants reproduce with seeds.) To form seeds, a plant's pollen grains (the male reproductive cells) must make contact with its ovules (the female reproductive cells). Plants can't pollinate themselves. Wind and water sometimes move pollen around, but most plants rely on animals such as insects, birds, and bats to do the job.

Animals visit plants to get food—either pollen grains or nectar, the sweet liquid plants make. For example, orchids in Madagascar have a scent that attracts sphinx moths. The moths drink nectar from the orchids. Pollen smears onto the moths. When the moths fly to other orchids, they spread the pollen on those plants.

Different rain forest plants attract different pollinators. Plants with bright colors and cup-shaped flowers often draw birds. Bats, the largest of the pollinators, seek plants with plenty of nectar to drink. Flies find flowers that smell like mildew or rot. Colorful red and orange flowers attract butterflies.

17

Rain forest relationships don't always involve plant reproduction. For example, the Amazonian cecropia tree has a hollow trunk and branches divided into chambers. Azteca ants live in these chambers. They eat the nectar the tree makes under its leaves. For their part, the ants defend the tree from other animals and plants. They bite and sting any animal that tries to eat the leaves, and they clip any vines trying to climb the trunk or branches. They also give the tree nutrients from frass (dead ants and other debris) that they leave behind.

RESOURCES FROM THE RAIN FOREST

In addition to absorbing carbon dioxide, recycling water, and preventing soil erosion, rain forests give humans many useful and necessary resources. Rain forests benefit not only the people who live in them but also humans throughout the world.

People eat many fruits and nuts from rain forest trees. They also use wood, oils, and resins (sticky, saplike liquids from trees and plants). For example, people harvest Brazil nuts and rubber from the Amazon rain forest. People make rattan furniture from the wood of palm trees in Indonesia and the Philippines.

Many rain forest trees make a milky sap called latex, a key ingredient in rubber.

Another important human benefit from rain forests is medicine. Over thousands of years, rain forest people have learned how to use the chemicals in local plants to meet their needs. People in Southeast Asian forests have used sixty-five hundred different plant species medicinally. Amazonian people have used thirteen hundred plant species for medicine.

For example, the Wapishana people of Guyana and Brazil have long used tipir (the nut of the greenheart tree) to stop bleeding and prevent infections, as well as for birth control. They also use the leaves of cunani bushes to paralyze the fish they want to catch. A scientist named Conrad Gorinsky has studied both plants. He's identified a chemical in tipir that reduces fever, prevents malaria relapses, and can be used to treat cancer and AIDS. In cunani leaves, he's found a chemical that can stimulate nerves and muscles to reverse heart blockage.

Like Gorinsky, researchers with more than one hundred companies worldwide are studying rain forest plants—and animals—that local people use medicinally. They're trying to identify the chemicals inside these organisms that perform certain tasks. If scientists can find these chemicals, they might be able to create similar ones in their labs.

In addition to foods, useful materials, and medicines, rain forests furnish another very important resource for humans. They provide water for the animals and people living in and near them. For example, the El Yunque rain forest in Puerto Rico furnishes one-third of the island's fresh drinking water.

DANGER: DEFORESTATION

About one-half of Earth's original rain forests—especially easy-to-reach lowland forests—are gone. Every year, people cut, burn, or otherwise destroy about 40 million acres (16 million hectares) of rain forest. That much forest would cover the entire state of Georgia. If deforestation continues at this rate, 25 percent of the Amazon forest could vanish by 2020. And 30 percent of the Congo forest could disappear by 2030.

These logs from a rain forest in Gabon await export.

Why do people destroy rain forests? The world's population has grown very quickly since the early 1900s. More people need more room to live and more food to eat. They also want more things to use in their daily lives. To meet their demands, they often clear rain forests.

Many of the people who live in and near rain forests are poor. In fact, many countries that lie within rain forest areas are poor. People in these areas have few resources to help them survive besides the forest itself. Companies from all over the world pay these people or countries to log,

FOREST RICHES

U.S., Japanese, and European companies destroy more rain forest than other companies. These companies' countries are rich. Rich countries demand more goods. Their willingness to pay for rain forest products adds to the problem of deforestation.

mine, ranch, and farm the forest. Their governments allow this deforestation because they hope the business that comes from it will improve their citizens' lives.

Deforestation causes both local and global damage. At least half of Earth's ten million species live in rain forests. If rain forest loss continues at its current rate, up to one-third of rain forest species could go extinct (die out) by 2040. That means deforestation could wipe out about one-sixth of Earth's species.

TOXIC SPILL

The Cofan people of Ecuador say that since the 1960s, an oil company has spilled 18 billion gallons (68 billion liters) of crude oil and poisonous waste onto their land and water and destroyed their forest home. A 1989 oil spill in the ocean near Alaska angered many people because it was so large. The spill in Ecuador is thirty times bigger than the Alaskan oil spill.

Rain forest residents at risk include thousands of humans. In some forests, most of the people who once thrived are gone.

Deforestation not only deprives local residents of their homes. It also upsets local ecosystems. It changes the land and the weather.

Rain forest loss can cause floods. A healthy forest soaks up lots of rainwater. When people clear the forest, rain flows quickly into rivers, taking tons of soil with it. These muddy rivers flood towns and fields. They destroy buildings, ruin farms, and take many lives. Erosion strips the soil of precious nutrients.

Deforestation can also cause long periods of dry weather called droughts. When people clear trees, they disturb the local rain cycle. The area absorbs less water, so it also releases less water vapor through transpiration. The drier air forms fewer clouds, and the area gets less rain. Droughts reduce supplies of drinking water and harm food production. They also increase the chance of wildfires.

This satellite photo shows fires in the temperate rain forest of southern Australia sending smoke far out to sea.

The loss of rain forests hurts not only nearby communities but all life on Earth. Rain forests absorb and store huge amounts of carbon dioxide from the atmosphere. When people destroy rain forests, they release that carbon dioxide into the air. They also destroy a resource that can store carbon dioxide humans produce in the future.

The amount of carbon dioxide in the air used to be stable. For more than half a million years, it held steady at about 280 parts per million (280 parts of carbon dioxide per one million parts of atmosphere). But since the 1800s, it has increased by about one-third. Our modern atmosphere contains about 382 parts per million of carbon dioxide—and this level is rising.

This growing amount of carbon dioxide is trapping more and more heat in our atmosphere. Like greenhouse windows, atmospheric carbon dioxide lets in the sun's light and traps its heat near the ground. A stable amount of carbon dioxide and other greenhouse gases in our atmosphere keeps Earth's temperature stable. But an increasing amount of carbon dioxide in the atmosphere causes Earth to slowly but steadily warm up.

This warming affects wind patterns and ocean currents, and these changes alter regional weather conditions. In some regions, the weather is becoming drier, leading to droughts and wildfires. In other regions, rainfall is increasing, leading to flooding. Studies suggest that global warming is probably making hurricanes stronger. In a few regions, the weather is growing colder due to changes in wind direction.

Weather changes are affecting the habitats (natural homes) of plants and animals all over the world. Some organisms can adjust to changes in their habitat or find new places to live, but others can't. Every day dozens of species go extinct. At the same time, climate change is improving living conditions for other creatures. For example, insects that carry deadly diseases like malaria are increasing in some areas.

As Earth gets warmer, much of its ice is melting. The ice sheets surrounding the North Pole and South Pole are slowly disappearing. Polar ice melt raises ocean levels, which threatens flooding in coastal areas. Some of the world's smaller islands might disappear completely. According to scientists, up to two thousand islands in Indonesia might vanish beneath the rising ocean.

Global warming is also melting mountain glaciers. Water from the melted ice causes rivers to overflow and flood places where people and animals live. Vanishing glaciers pose another problem too. Glaciers provide millions of people around the world with freshwater to drink. Without those glaciers, people will need to find other sources of water.

Global warming is a very serious problem. And deforestation contributes to this problem. Saving our planet's rain forests is a critical part of the solution.

CHAPTER TWO

RAIN FORESTS
OF THE AMERICAS

The Western Hemisphere does not have as much land as the Eastern Hemisphere. However, the Americas are rich in rain forests. The continents of North and South America are home to the world's largest tropical and temperate rain forests.

AMERICAN TROPICAL RAIN FORESTS

The Western Hemisphere's tropical rain forests grow in Mexico, Central America, the Caribbean, and South America. The largest rain forest in the world is South America's Amazon forest.

The Amazon rain forest covers an area almost four times the size of Alaska.

This tropical rain forest covers approximately 2.3 million square miles (6 million square kilometers). That's almost four times the size of Alaska. Most of the Amazon is in Brazil. It also includes parts of Suriname, Guyana, French Guiana, Venezuela, Peru, Bolivia, Ecuador, and Colombia. One-quarter of the world's freshwater cycles through the Amazon forest. More than three hundred different groups of forest people live there.

The Amazon is the most biodiverse region in the world. One-third of Earth's species live there. These species include more than 56,000 kinds of plants,

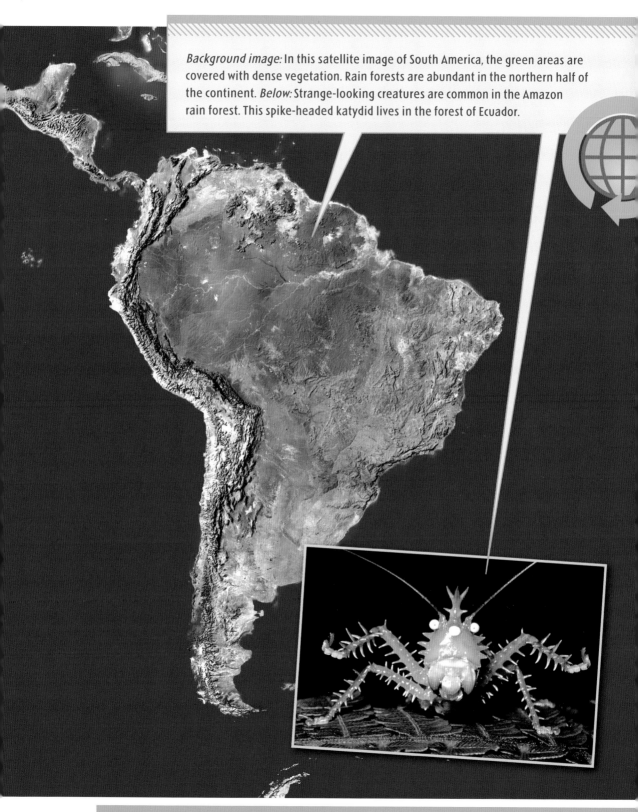

Background image: In this satellite image of South America, the green areas are covered with dense vegetation. Rain forests are abundant in the northern half of the continent. *Below:* Strange-looking creatures are common in the Amazon rain forest. This spike-headed katydid lives in the forest of Ecuador.

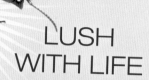

LUSH WITH LIFE

In South America's tropical rain forests, nearly five hundred types of trees might grow in only 2.5 acres (1 hectare) of forest. In Peru, scientists found that a section of trees about the size of a two-car garage contained more than one hundred thousand individual invertebrates. (Invertebrates are animals without backbones, such as insects, spiders, worms, and snails.) One single tree in the Amazon held ninety-five kinds of ants.

1,700 bird species, 695 kinds of amphibians, 578 mammal species, and 651 kinds of reptiles.

The Amazon's plant population is especially impressive. About twenty-five hundred different tree species grow there. Nearly thirty thousand Amazon plant species grow nowhere else on Earth. Among these species is the world's largest water lily, the Victoria water lily. Its leaves can grow over 9 feet (3 m) in diameter.

Amazonian animals are many and varied too. Jaguars, harpy eagles, and giant river otters run, fly, and swim through the region. Pygmy marmosets (a kind of monkey) spend their days scooping tasty sap from beneath tree bark. Their energetic relatives, the tamarins, scurry and jump around them. Sloths hang sleepily in the canopy.

In the Andes (a South American mountain range that extends into the Amazon), the Bolivian mountain coconut palm grows at altitudes of up to 11,100 feet (3,400 m). That's higher than any other palm tree on Earth. Earth's largest bromeliad, a relative of the pineapple, also lives there. *Puya raimondii* can grow up to 40 feet (12 m) tall when it's flowering. It's Earth's slowest-growing plant,

RAIN CATCHERS

Some bromeliads can hold more than 2 gallons (8 liters) of rainwater in pools among their leaves. One giant species can hold 8 gallons (30 liters) of rainwater. Millions of creatures that live in the rain forest canopy drink water from these pools. Tiny frog tadpoles even swim in them.

taking about one hundred years to mature.

On the western slopes of the Andes lies the Chocó region. It includes parts of Panama, Colombia, and Ecuador. This rain forest region is home to many plants with huge leaves. *Psittacanthus gigas*, the world's largest-leafed plant, grows there. Its leaves can reach up to 3.3 feet (1 m) long and 1.6 feet (0.5 m) wide.

THE VANISHING AMAZON

The Amazon rain forest is steadily shrinking. It loses about 13,382 square miles (34,660 sq. km) every year. That's an area larger than the state of Maryland. People have destroyed almost 20 percent of the Amazon.

Much of this deforestation is clearing to make pastures for cattle grazing. Ranchers raise cattle for meat and sell it around the world. In the 1970s, Amazon ranchers sold about 40 percent of their meat to Europe. Thirty years later, Europeans buy 74 percent of Amazon ranchers' beef.

Cattle in Panama graze on land that used to be covered in rain forest.

28

Many poor farmers have cleared the Amazon too. In Brazil, farmers can get public rain forest land for free by living on it for five years. Poor farmers move into the forest to improve their lives. They clear the trees and plant bananas, palms, corn, soybeans, or rice. The poor soil supports these crops for one or two years. The farmers then move to new plots of land. They either abandon the old land or turn it into cattle pasture.

In the 1970s, Brazil built a major highway through the Amazon. The Trans-Amazonian Highway made it easier for people to travel deep into the forest. They could log more trees and clear more land for farms and cattle ranches. Before 1970 people had destroyed about 2.5 percent of the forest. Since 1970 the Amazon rain forest has shrunk about 15 percent.

Farmers and ranchers usually clear rain forest by burning it. Sometimes their fires blaze out of control, burning down large areas of forest. Fires also add carbon dioxide to the air.

TERRA PRETA

Ancient Amazonians created a nutrient-rich soil called *terra preta*. They added charcoal and ground animal bones to the soil. This increased the minerals in soil. It helped the soil hold moisture. It helped plants grow and kept soil fertile for a long time.

The recipe for terra preta disappeared thousands of years ago, along with its makers. But scientists are trying to figure it out. With terra preta, a rain forest farmer could stay on one plot of land. This might help reduce deforestation. It also could help poor countries make more money.

Laws limit the amount of logging people can do in Brazil. But illegal logging continues anyway. Flooding from hydroelectric dams (dams that produce electricity by waterpower) and mining for gold also add to Amazon deforestation.

ANIMALS AT RISK

As the rain forest disappears, animals lose their homes. The noise and commotion of logging, mining, and road construction also scare away animals.

Dozens of Amazonian animal species are endangered (at risk of going extinct). Among these are the giant armadillo and several kinds of lion tamarins. Many species of sloths, opossums, marmosets, otters, and other creatures are in danger of dying out too.

For example, jaguars once lived all the way from the southwestern United States to Argentina. In the early twenty-first century, they live only in parts of the Amazon. Once four hundred thousand charcoal monkeys lived in Brazil. They've lost much of their habitat. Fewer than six hundred remain.

Amphibians are disappearing worldwide—including from the tropical rain

A pair of golden toads from a protected forest in Costa Rica mate in an aquarium before being returned to the wild. This species of toad is now believed to be extinct.

forests of the Americas. In the first few years of the twenty-first century, more than twenty species went extinct. Among them was Costa Rica's golden toad. Scientists discovered this toad in 1964. Nobody has seen one since 1989.

Shrinking animal populations affect more than the animals themselves. When one species dwindles or dies out, its loss can endanger other living things that depend on it. For example, the Amazonian Zam tree depends on one type of butterfly to pollinate it. The butterfly has a tongue just the right size to fit into the Zam tree's flowers. The pollinated tree produces hard seeds that fall to the forest floor. The agouti, a small rodent, eats the seeds with its sharp teeth. The agouti also stores seeds, which later grow into new Zam trees. Some ants feed only on the Zam tree's leaves. One kind of lizard eats only these ants and the butterfly that pollinates the tree. A certain tree snake eats the lizard. Other animals, such as jaguars, eat agoutis.

If the butterfly goes extinct, the Zam tree will too. Then the agouti and the ants will follow. Jaguars that eat the agoutis, lizards that eat the ants and butterflies, and tree snakes that eat the lizards will lose an important source of food.

PEOPLE IN PERIL

People living in American tropical rain forests once thrived by hunting animals and gathering plant foods. They moved from place to place in search of better hunting and new plants to eat. They wore clothes made from forest animals or plants. They knew which plants to avoid and which they could use as medicine. Sometimes they farmed. Many knew how to clear trees in a way that didn't damage the forest.

As trees disappear, forest people lose their means of survival. They lose many of the animals they hunt and the plants they gather for food and clothing. Some forget their forest skills. Their communities lose track of traditional knowledge, such as how to use medicinal plants and how to farm the forest without hurting it. They may even lose their lives. Sometimes outsiders who come to work and live in the forest bring deadly diseases with them.

A Huaorani man hunts using traditional methods. A clan, or family, of the Huaorani called the Tageri are in danger of losing their homeland in Ecuador to oil drilling.

FOREST CULTURE

The Tageri people of Ecuador are hunters and gatherers who move from place to place. They're among the few rain forest peoples who still live according to the old ways. But companies want to drill for oil in their territory. The Tageri are fighting fiercely to preserve their land and culture.

Deforestation is forcing forest people to change their ways. They no longer hunt and gather. They still farm, but they grow food, such as bananas, for sale to outsiders instead of for their own needs. They buy and sell products at nearby markets. They wear the same kinds of clothes worn by people in the United States and Europe. Many sell crafts to tourists to earn money.

With these changes, the people lose their distinct sense of self, or identity. They no longer understand their own culture. They also can lose important knowledge that helps them survive in their environment.

AMERICAN TEMPERATE RAIN FORESTS

The Western Hemisphere is home to most of the world's temperate rain forests. This type of rain forest grows along the Pacific coasts of South and North America.

South America's temperate rain forest lies in Chile and Argentina. It blankets the

Mosses and epiphytes coat these trees in the temperate rain forest of Olympic National Park in Washington.

western slopes of mountains in areas called the Valdivian and Magellanic forests. These areas contain about 20 percent of Earth's temperate rain forests. They make up the second-largest temperate rain forest in the world. About one-third of the trees and vines growing there live nowhere else in the world. More than thirty-five mammal species live there. These include one of the world's smallest deer and South America's smallest cat.

This rare spirit bear is fishing for a meal in British Columbia, Canada.

North America's temperate rain forest runs from northern California through British Columbia, Canada, into Alaska. This area is the world's largest tract of such forest. It makes up about 50 percent of the temperate rain forest left on Earth. It is home to about 350 animal species, including the rare spirit bear, a type of black bear that has white fur. Among this forest's twenty-five tree species are some of the oldest, tallest trees in the world.

Coastal temperate rain forests once grew on every continent except Africa and Antarctica. They covered about 1 percent of Earth's land. People have destroyed more than half of that small amount.

Of the rain forests that once grew in California, Oregon, and Washington, 95 percent have vanished. More than 50 percent of British Columbia's rain forest is gone. More than 10 percent of Alaska's is gone too. The vast majority of surviving temperate rain forest is in the Americas. New Zealand has preserved a little, but almost none is left in Europe and Asia.

CHAPTER THREE

RAIN FORESTS OF AFRICA, ASIA, AND OCEANIA

The lands of the Eastern Hemisphere—Africa, Europe, Asia, and Oceania—are home to the world's oldest rain forests. Much of the planet's worst deforestation is found here too.

AFRICAN RAIN FORESTS

About 20 percent of the world's rain forests grow in Africa's Congo River basin. This area is Earth's second-largest tropical rain forest. It covers nearly 1.5 million square miles (3.9 million sq. km). It stretches from central Africa west

34

More than ten thousand animal species and six hundred tree species live in the Congo rain forest.

to the Atlantic coast. It grows in Rwanda, Burundi, Democratic Republic of Congo, Central African Republic, Republic of the Congo, Cameroon, Gabon, and Equatorial Guinea.

The Congo rain forest is home to many different kinds of living things. More than ten thousand animal species and six hundred tree species live there. Among Africa's most famous rain forest animals are apes and elephants. Chimpanzees, bonobos, and gorillas live in the Congo. So do most of Africa's forest elephants.

Background image: The deepest green area on this satellite image is the Congo rain forest in central Africa. Animals such as this mountain gorilla *(left)* live in Africa's rain forests.

AFRICAN FOREST ELEPHANTS

Scientists call African forest elephants *(below)* "engineers of the rain forest" because they help shape the habitat for other species. The elephants maintain a vast network of trails linking their favorite fruit trees and *bais* (salty marshes). They gather at bais to socialize, eat, drink, and dig for mineral salts.

As the elephants go about their lives, they eat leaves and shoots, knock down trees, and trample undergrowth. These actions let more sunlight into the forest. They create open areas that draw other species. The elephants also dig with their tusks, shatter rotting logs, and leave dung behind wherever they go. These actions loosen the soil, add nutrients to it, and spread plant seeds throughout the forest.

Several groups of forest people live in the Congo. They are short people—usually less than 5 feet (1.5 m) tall. Many of them move from place to place and survive by hunting and gathering. (Some forest people also plant small crops or trade with nearby villagers.) When they settle in a new place, they clear away undergrowth and small trees. They leave the big canopy trees standing to provide shade. When the people move away, small trees and other plants grow back quickly.

Human destruction of the African rain forest has increased since the 1980s. During this time, the Congo has shrunk by about 11 percent. Farming causes the most Congo deforestation.

Workers at a diamond mine in the Democratic Republic of Congo dig through layers of mud and rock in search of diamonds. Disturbing the land means destroying the delicate balance of life that depends on it.

Logging in the Congo has grown during the early twenty-first century. Logging provides jobs for thousands of people. Some of these people have no other way to earn money. It also offers low-paid government workers a way to earn extra money. Companies secretly pay these workers to allow illegal logging.

People mine diamonds and drill for oil in the Congo too. Logging and mining roads make it easier for people to travel deep into the forest. Some people clear land for farming. Others, called poachers, use the roads for illegal hunting. They sell the meat to loggers, miners, and nearby villagers. They also hunt elephants for their ivory tusks.

Since the 1990s, civil wars in central Africa have added to rain forest destruction. Hundreds of thousands of refugees have fled to the forest to escape violence. More people living in the forest bring more damage to its plants and wildlife.

Violence has spilled into the forest too. For example, attacks have occurred in the Virunga Mountains—a rain forest area in Uganda, Rwanda, and the Democratic Republic of Congo. All of Earth's seven hundred or so mountain

Game wardens in a national park in the Central African Republic inspect an elephant killed by poachers. The poachers had removed its tusks and left the body to rot in a stream.

gorillas live there, mainly in national parks. So far, about 120 park rangers have died protecting the endangered gorillas and the forest. An unknown number of gorillas have also died.

As more people move into Africa's rain forests for various reasons, the forest people get crowded out. They lose their trees to loggers. They lose their game (the animals they hunt and eat legally) to poachers and to noisy machines that scare away animals. Many must hunt illegally or find other ways to survive.

ASIAN RAIN FORESTS

Asia's tropical rain forests grow in southern and Southeast Asia. They're found in Sri Lanka, southern India, Myanmar, Vietnam, Laos, Cambodia, Thailand, Malaysia, the Philippines, and Indonesia. Their trees are mostly from the dipterocarp family. Almost four hundred species from this family grow in Asian rain forests.

Southeast Asian rain forests are among the oldest in the world. Some Malaysian forests might be one hundred million years old. That's about four hundred times older than the human race.

Asia's largest rain forest lies in a group of Southeast Asian islands known as the Indonesian archipelago. More than seventeen thousand islands cover about 1 million square miles (2.6 million sq. km) between mainland Asia and Australia. Three of the biggest islands are Borneo, Sumatra, and Java.

This area includes many different kinds of ecological regions. These regions, or ecoregions, share similar land, climate, and living things. Each ecoregion in this area is very biodiverse. For example, tigers, rhinoceroses, orangutans, and

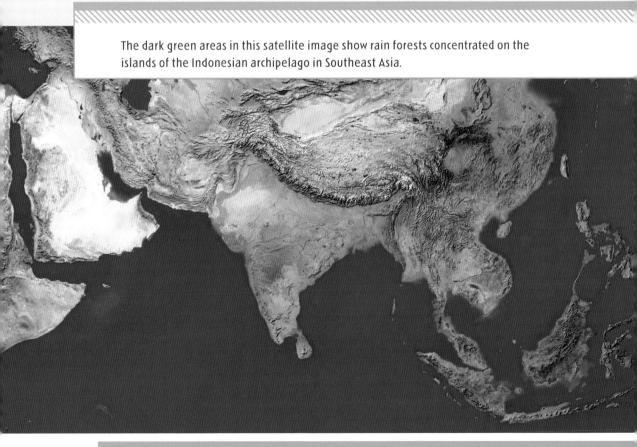

The dark green areas in this satellite image show rain forests concentrated on the islands of the Indonesian archipelago in Southeast Asia.

elephants all live on Borneo. This island is the only place in the world where all these animals live together.

Many Southeast Asian species are endemic. They live in this region and nowhere else in the world. About 31 percent of Indonesia's 3,305 animal species are endemic. So are almost 60 percent of Indonesia's 29,375 plant species.

Borneo and Sumatra are especially biodiverse. At least 15,000 plant species grow on Borneo. About 6,000 of them are endemic. Since the early 1980s, scientists have discovered 422 new plant species there. In Sumatra's Tesso Nilo forest, scientists found 218 plant species in a plot of land covering only 2,100 square feet (195 sq. m). That's more species per square foot (0.1 sq. m) than any other place on Earth.

Rain forests are disappearing from Southeast Asia faster than from any other part of the world. Logging has damaged the forests. Logging also puts forests at greater risk for fire.

BABY ORANGUTANS

Many people want baby orangutans as pets. Poachers steal them from rain forests. Mother orangutans usually die trying to protect their babies. Sometimes babies die falling from trees. Other baby orangutans die after they're captured, either from human diseases or from poor treatment.

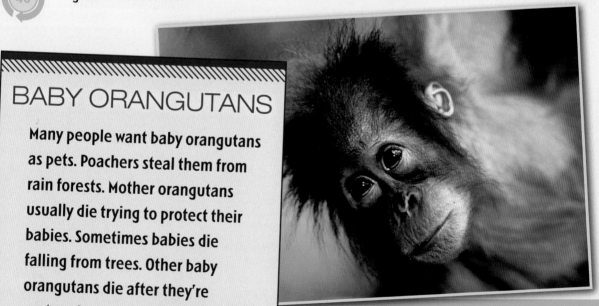

This baby orangutan lives in the Gunung Leuser National Park of Indonesia.

Indonesian villagers fight wildfires with tree branches. Droughts in Indonesia left dry vegetation that burned readily.

In the early 1990s, a very large fire burned the rain forest in Borneo. An unusually warm ocean current created conditions that led to a severe drought in the area. (These warm currents in the Pacific Ocean happen every few years. This event is known as El Niño.) The warm water created winds that blew away Borneo's usual rain clouds. This dried out the forest, which was already dry due to logging. When people burned trees to clear land for farming, the fires blew out of control. More than 15,500 square miles (25,000 sq. km) of rain forest burned down.

Political unrest in Southeast Asian countries has also damaged many forests. Officials in violent areas are unable or unwilling to enforce laws protecting the environment.

Overcrowding is a big problem in many Asian countries too. People are moving from cities and towns into rain forest areas. They're cutting trees for fuel and building material.

Workers at a rubber tree plantation on Java, Indonesia, prepare to tap trees. Plantations have replaced natural rain forests in many areas of the country.

Rain forests once covered almost three-quarters of Borneo. Much of the island was so thickly forested that people couldn't move through it at all. In the 1980s and 1990s, people cut down one-third of the island's forests to make plywood for use in building homes. They also farmed the lands to grow and export rubber and palm oil.

Most of Sumatra was once covered with tropical rain forest. Only 15 percent of its original forest remains. Logging and farming have wiped out the rest.

Deforestation in Asia is destroying the habitat of some of the continent's most fascinating animals. Orangutans once lived throughout Asia. They are Earth's largest tree-living mammal and the only great ape that lives outside Africa. Orangutans have lost about 80 percent of their habitat since the 1950s. Their numbers have dropped by more than 50 percent since the 1980s. They remain only in parts of Borneo and Sumatra. They are severely endangered.

Like the orangutan, the tiger once roamed all over Asia. It lived throughout the continent from India to Siberia to Southeast Asia. Deforestation and poaching have caused three out of eight tiger subspecies to go extinct. Poachers hunt tigers for their body parts, which are ground up for use in Chinese medicine. The Sumatran tiger is the only tiger left in all of Indonesia. Only five hundred of these tigers remain, all on Sumatra.

Sumatran and Javan rhinoceroses are almost extinct from habitat loss and hunting. They once lived throughout Southeast Asia but now live only in the Indonesian archipelago. Fewer than three hundred Sumatran rhinos and fewer than one hundred Javan rhinos remain. As with tigers, poachers hunt rhinos for their body parts.

Borneo's pygmy elephants, too, are critically endangered. Fewer than one thousand of these elephants remain on Earth.

The people who used to live in Asian rain forests now live in only a few areas. They live very deep inside some forests in Sri Lanka, India's Andaman Islands,

Endangered species such as the Sumatran rhinoceros *(left)* and the pygmy elephant of Borneo *(right)* are disappearing as their forest homelands shrink.

The Penan people of Borneo rely on their rain forest home. Here they extract a type of flour from the sago palm. The palm also provides material for housing and weaving baskets.

mainland Malaysia, the island of Borneo, and the Philippines. For example, only a few thousand of the Vedda people remain in Sri Lanka. About four hundred Jarawa people remain in the Andaman forests.

These and other Asian forest people are losing not only their land but also their cultures. They're losing the ability to live in harmony with the rain forest. Worst of all, thousands of them are losing their lives.

RAIN FORESTS OF OCEANIA

Oceania is the region of the world lying south and east of Asia. It includes the continent of Australia. It also includes more than ten thousand Pacific islands. Some of these islands, such as New Guinea and New Zealand's North and South Islands, are large. Others, such as Samoa, Fiji, and the Hawaiian Islands, are small.

New Guinea is Earth's biggest tropical island. Its western half belongs to Indonesia. The eastern half is a separate country called Papua New Guinea. Tropical rain forest covers about 65 percent of Papua New Guinea. This forest is the third-largest rain forest left in the world.

VITAL BATS

Bats pollinate many kinds of plants. They're the only animals that can pollinate kapok, eucalyptus, durian, mango, clove, banana, guava, avocado, breadfruit, ebony, mahogany, and cashew trees. Bats pollinate most of the forests in Southeast Asia and Oceania. If bats die out, these forests will too.

This black flying fox lives in Queensland, Australia.

In Australia, rain forests grow in the Kimberley region of Western Australia and across the Northern Territory. Many fruits attract pollinating birds and flying foxes (large bats) in these forests.

Two small areas of rain forest grow in the Cape York Peninsula in Queensland in northeastern Australia. They are the oldest continually living rain forests in the world. Twelve of Earth's nineteen original flowering plant families live in these forests. Up to 120 different tree species grow in 2.5 acres (1 hectare) of the Cape York forests.

Rain forests also grow on the eastern coast of Australia, through New South Wales and Victoria. In New South Wales, 75 percent of the original forests have disappeared since the 1500s. About 1.2 million acres (486,000 hectares) of rain forest remain.

About 1.5 million acres (598,000 hectares) of rain forests grow on the southeastern Australian island of Tasmania. These include temperate rain forests as well as tropical ones. They cover 10 percent of the island. Many of the plants and animals in Tasmania are endemic. More than six hundred of these species are threatened.

Tropical rain forests grow on most of the thousands of tiny islands in the Pacific Ocean. Many of these islands are still thickly forested. But the islands are so tiny that their total amount of forest doesn't add up to much.

These islands are isolated, surrounded by oceans too vast for easy travel. For this reason, the island plants and animals evolved differently than those of many other areas on Earth. A large percentage of them are endemic. Up to one-third of the species of these islands live nowhere else on Earth.

A panandas tree grows tall in the rain forest of Papua New Guinea.

The rain forest of New Guinea contains Oceania's greatest variety of living things. More than eleven thousand plant species grow there, and 60 percent of them are endemic. This forest is also home to 1,571 animal species. About 25 percent of them are endemic.

Australia's rain forests contain more than fifteen thousand plant species, 90 percent of them endemic. Some of the trees are more than three thousand years old. About one-third of Australia's mammals live in its rain forests. About one-quarter of Australia's reptiles and nearly half of its bird species live there too.

Much of New Guinea's rain forest still remains. But every year, people clear about 193 square miles (500 sq. km) of it.

Since the late 1700s, when Europeans began settling in Australia, people have cleared 75 percent of Australia's tropical rain forest. Rain forest covers only 16,216 square miles (41,999 sq. km) of the continent today. This is less than 1 percent of Australia's land.

In the Pacific islands, farming and construction reduced the forests slowly over time. But in modern times, logging has reduced the forests much faster. Cocoa, palm, and coconut plantations also add to deforestation.

Hundreds of thousands of native people lived in Australia's rain forests before Europeans began arriving there. The continent's rain forests were hard to reach. It took longer for outsiders to arrive there than in other rain forests around the world. When they did arrive, the outsiders changed both the forests and the people living in them.

More than half the native people of Australia died once Europeans settled in the country in the 1700s and 1800s. Most died of smallpox and other diseases.

Australia's forest people have kept their languages alive. They still understand the plants and systems of their forests. But they struggle against deforestation and settlement by outsiders. Many have been forced off their lands and moved to cities or other communities.

NEW ZEALAND'S FOREST TREASURE

New Zealand's temperate rain forest is one of only five major temperate rain forests in the world. Along the western coast grows one of only three major southern beech forests on Earth. Among New Zealand's unusual forest animals are the flightless takahe bird, the Fiordland crested penguin, and the kea parrot.

CHAPTER FOUR

SAVING RAIN FORESTS FOR A HEALTHIER EARTH

Around the world, people are working to save rain forests. Consumers, farmers, loggers, scientists, students, and forest people are asking questions and seeking answers. Environmental groups are bringing together people and resources.

Governments in rain forest countries are writing new laws. They hope these laws will strengthen their forests and people. Governments in other countries are also drafting new laws.

In 1989 a group called the International Labor Organization (ILO) created a new agreement called ILO Convention 169. It says that indigenous (native) and tribal people have the right to exist and to keep their distinctive identities. It also says that these people may decide if, how, and when to develop their land. By 2007 nineteen countries—including fourteen rain forest nations—had ratified ILO 169.

HELPING RAIN FORESTS IN THE AMERICAS

Many projects are helping rain forests in the Americas. These projects bring together different groups of people to protect many different regions.

For example, the World Wildlife Fund (WWF) has developed two new protected areas in Brazil's Amazon. They include 9.4 million acres (3.8 million hectares) of rain forest. This is almost as big as the state of South Carolina. The areas protect jaguars, macaws, harpy eagles, and other threatened species.

The WWF areas are part of a larger project called the Amazon Region Protected Areas (ARPA). The WWF, the World Bank, and the government of Brazil

Background image: A member of Africa's Ba'Aka people hunts for food in Cameroon. Rain forest people around the world risk losing their ways of life as rain forests shrink. Governments and conservation groups, such as the World Wildlife Federation, are working together to prevent this loss. *Below:* Panelists speak at a WWF conference.

sponsor this larger project. The full ARPA area is bigger than the state of California. The project includes plans for a system of national parks and other protected lands. The first of the parks—the Tumucumaque Mountains National Park in Brazil— opened in 2002. It is the world's largest tropical forest national park.

The Nature Conservancy (NC) Adopt an Acre program protects more than 600,000 acres (242,811 hectares) of rain forests globally. The NC helped Costa Rica create a national park in 1975. The NC continues to work with other groups, including Conservation International (CI), to protect rain forests in Costa Rica. These groups are developing a corridor, or path, of protected land between national parks. The corridor will provide protected habitat for animals that need large spaces to survive.

La Amistad International Peace Park *(below)* spans parts of Costa Rica and Panama. Other parks and protected areas lie next to La Amistad, expanding the safe habitat for a variety of species, such as the scarlet macaw *(inset)*.

Other efforts are afoot to save rain forests throughout the Americas. In Chile a businessman worked with the NC to buy and protect coastal temperate rain forest land. In the United States, many groups are meeting to discuss how to protect Alaska's temperate rain forest. The meetings include groups that disagree on forest use, such as lumber companies, fisheries, the NC, native people, and government agencies. In 2005 the United States passed a new law. This law protects 10,000 acres (4,047 hectares) of El Yunque rain forest in Puerto Rico. Other projects aim to protect specific animal species. CI projects protect the jaguar, scarlet macaw, and Central American river turtle.

Still other projects help forest people. In Guyana the Wai Wai people gained ownership of 1.5 million acres (607,028 hectares) of rain forest land. They met with the government of Guyana and asked for legal ownership of this land. In

SMART LOGGING

New logging methods can help companies avoid wasting timber. For example, workers can build roads so that they destroy as few trees as possible. Methods like these are called sustainable forestry. Sustainable forestry can produce the same amount of timber as old logging methods with half the amount of cut trees.

In 1941 California's Collins Almanor forest held 1.5 billion board feet (3.5 million cu. m) of standing timber. (Board feet is a measurement of lumber volume. A board foot is equal to 144 cubic inches [2,360 cu. cm] of wood.) Then sustainable forestry began there. In 2001 the forest provided 2 billion board feet (4.7 million cu. m) of wood. But it still held 1.5 billion board feet (3.5 million cu. m) of standing timber.

51

RAIN FOREST TRAINING

In 2006 a group of Amazonian forest people and the Nature Conservancy created the Amazon Indigenous Training Center. This center, known locally as CAFI, trains young native people in forest conservation. They learn how to track and map forest activities and how to manage natural resources. They also learn about environmental laws. They can use this knowledge to protect and restore their rain forest lands.

2004 the government signed an agreement with them. It was the first time in Guyana that forest people officially owned their own land. Their land is now known as the Wai Wai Community Owned Conservation Area.

The Wai Wai have joined with CI to plan ways to protect the rain forest. The Wai Wai manage efforts to protect their land, and they work to keep families together there.

In Brazil, CI worked with a Brazilian group called NGO Fundação SOS Mata Atlântica. Together these groups helped local landowners create protected areas in the Atlantic Forest.

CI and Bunge, Brazil's largest soybean company, work with soybean farmers. They teach the farmers how to use fewer pesticides. They also suggest better ways to water crops and prevent soil erosion. These efforts have helped farmers better use and protect rain forest lands.

HELPING RAIN FORESTS IN AFRICA

In recent years, governments and international groups have come together to help save Africa's rain forests. Working with the WWF, central African leaders met in Yaoundé, Cameroon, in 1999. They wrote the Yaoundé Declaration. In this plan,

52

they agreed to create an 8.6 million-acre (3.5 million-hectare) wilderness in the Central African Republic, Cameroon, and the Republic of the Congo. Leaders from all three of these countries agreed to this plan. The plan also created laws to prevent illegal loggers and poachers from crossing borders to escape capture.

The later Congo Basin Forest Partnership (CBFP) protects millions of acres of African rain forest. Among these protected lands are thirteen new parks in Gabon. This partnership brings together leaders of countries and international groups to help work to better manage Congo Basin rain forests.

At the 2002 Earth Summit in South Africa, Gabon agreed to create a national park system. It will protect 11 percent of the country's land.

Other projects help people in Africa's rain forests. The Ba'Aka people of Gabon's Minkebe forest worked with the WWF. They formed an organization called

The president of the Republic of the Congo *(right)* speaks to reporters during a 2002 meeting of the Congo Basin Forest Partnership. Colin Powell *(seated left)* of the United States helped launch the CBFP.

Edzengui. This Ba'Aka word means "spirit of the forest." Edzengui helps the Ba'Aka remain in and protect their rain forest home. An indigenous people, the Ba'Aka hunted and gathered food to survive. The Ba'Aka have no identity cards or other official documents. As a result, they often can't travel, go to school, get medicine, or even vote. They have little choice but to poach animals to survive. Edzengui helps the Ba'Aka find other ways to feed their families, such as forest-safe farming.

Since Edzengui formed, elephant poaching in the Minkebe forest has dropped. In 2001 poachers killed 104 elephants. In 2004 poachers killed only 50.

HELPING FORESTS IN ASIA AND OCEANIA

The WWF has also worked with local groups in Southeast Asia and Oceania. It helped create a community forum for people who live near Sumatra's Tesso Nilo National Park. This forum includes residents of twenty-two villages in the area. Members meet to find ways of earning money without harming the rain forest. Ecotourism and honey production are two such ways.

This forum also created the Tesso Nilo Flying Squads. These teams of domesticated (tame) elephants are trained to drive away wild elephants. Wild Sumatran elephants lost their habitat to deforestation. The elephants moved into farms seeking food and have destroyed houses and entire crops. People acted to protect their farms. They caught or killed these endangered elephants. The Tesso Nilo Flying Squads provide a way to protect both the farms and the elephants. In one village, crop damage dropped from forty-five hundred dollars per month to twenty-nine dollars per month when the squads began working.

In Papua New Guinea, the WWF delivered three thousand vanilla tree cuttings to three villages. The villagers can grow the cuttings into vanilla trees. They sell the vanilla beans for money instead of selling their forests to loggers. The villagers also share cuttings from their plants. This enables their neighbors to grow and sell vanilla beans too.

One of the Tesso Nilo Flying Squads of Sumatra patrols the jungle to protect local villages and farms from destruction by wild elephants.

PARTNERSHIPS FOR PROTECTION

Sometimes very different organizations or far-flung countries join to find new ways of improving Earth's health. Some of these partnerships have given birth to creative and effective ways of saving rain forests.

For example, governments and businesses that put too much carbon dioxide into the air can buy carbon credits from environmental groups. These groups then use the money for projects that remove carbon dioxide from the air. Sometimes people call carbon credits carbon offsets, because the credits offset (make up for) environmental damage.

Some experts believe carbon credits are a bad idea. They let companies and people with money keep pouring carbon into the air instead of changing their habits. But other experts argue that carbon credits are a good first step. They bring in money to find ideas and carry out projects that protect Earth.

Papua New Guinea and eight other rain forest countries have proposed a new use for carbon credits. Rain forest countries that reduce deforestation could earn and sell carbon credits. Many think this effort could encourage people to change their habits. It could provide people in rain forest areas a new way to earn money. They could sell carbon credits instead of cutting down trees. They could earn money by protecting their forests instead of harming them.

Sometimes businesses play a big role in rain forest conservation. For example, Starbucks Corporation, the National Federation of Coffee Growers of Colombia, and Conservation International have teamed up in Colombia. They teach coffee farmers farming methods that don't harm forests and wildlife. In Peru, CI and the cosmetics company Aveda Corporation work with local groups of forest people. They create businesses that harvest forest products without hurting the forest.

Sometimes businesses play a big role in rain forest conservation.

Many groups in Canada's Great Bear rain forest work to find ways for local people to both protect the land and earn money. The project includes environmental groups such as the Nature Conservancy and the Sierra Club of Canada. Timber companies, governments, and native forest people also work together in this project.

Rain forest partnerships can even reach across the globe. For example, Amazonians met with Canadians to discuss the Great Bear project. They learned what the Canadians are doing and how, so they can try these methods in the Amazon.

ON THE FRINGE

Some people come up with strange ideas to save rain forests. Some of these ideas work, and others don't. But all ideas help us think harder about how to preserve our forests.

For example, some people in the African country of Kenya raise butterflies. The butterfly farmers sell hundreds of butterflies at a time to Americans and Europeans. Some of the buyers are rich people, who release the butterflies at parties. Others are scientists who want to study the butterflies. The money goes to help Kenya's Kakamega forest. This forest is the easternmost remnant of the original Congo rain forest.

Many celebrities have ideas to save rain forests. They use their fame to educate and challenge people. Several famous musicians are in on the act.

A butterfly farmer in Malindi, Kenya, feeds fruit to one of his butterflies. Raising butterflies to sell helps Kenyans earn a living and protect the rain forest.

Singer Sheryl Crow advises slowing deforestation by using fewer paper products. She suggests that we each use less toilet paper. She challenges us to try using one square per visit. Crow also created shirts with "dining sleeves." One sleeve on each shirt is detachable. Users wipe their mouths on the removable sleeves instead of on paper napkins. Then they take off the sleeves and replace them. They can wash the dirty sleeves and use them again.

Other musicians try to set good examples for their fans. They try to treat Earth gently as they perform around the globe. By conserving fuel and other materials, they do their part to reduce deforestation for oil, food, and other products. They also spread the word about global warming and a healthy atmosphere.

In 2007 singer Sheryl Crow participated in a college tour to raise money and awareness about global warming. Crow and many other performers do their part to help protect the environment.

The Canadian band Barenaked Ladies is actively involved in saving the environment. Band members recycle their backstage materials and fuel their tour bus with biodeisel (a more Earth-friendly fuel than gasoline), among other things.

The rock group Barenaked Ladies, for example, has helpers gather its broken guitar strings after each concert. An artist recycles the strings into jewelry. This popular jewelry makes money for the environmental charity Barenaked Planet. The group's players also eat locally grown organic food wherever they travel. They drink from reusable containers instead of plastic disposable bottles. The band buys energy credits to offset the electricity it uses in its concerts. It also presents a slide show on global warming before each concert.

GOING GREEN

Chances are, you don't live in or near a rain forest. You may wonder how you can help protect Earth's rain forests from far away. Here are several things you can do:

- **Eat less beef.** It takes 12 pounds (5.4 kilograms) of grain and 2,500 gallons (9,461 liters) of water to produce 1 pound (0.5 kg) of hamburger. Land is often cleared to produce this grain and provide pastures. Cattle ranches are major sources of deforestation.

- **Use less paper.** Most paper comes from trees, so using less paper helps reduce logging. Use recycled paper made from 100 percent post-consumer waste (PCW). (PCW is used material collected by recycling programs.) Or use paper made not from trees but from other plant materials, such as kenaf fiber, cornstalks, or wheat straw. If paper is 100 percent PCW or tree-free, its package will say so.

- **Raise money for rain forests.** Help raise funds to support projects such as the Rainforest Action Network's Protect-an-Acre program:
  - Organize a music, theater, or poetry event. Pass a collection jar for donations.
  - Join forces with others from your classroom or neighborhood. Hold a rummage sale, host a popcorn or lemonade stand, have a car wash, or plan a bake sale.
  - Collect aluminum cans and recycle them for cash.

These kids paint a rain forest mural as a backdrop for a play to raise awareness about the rain forest.

- Hold a walkathon or bikeathon. Ask people to promise to give a certain amount of money for each mile you travel.
- Ask a parent, adult friend, or teacher to host a rain forest fund-raising party. Ask the host to serve foods and drinks made of organic or fair-trade foods from the rain forest.

• **Spread the word.** Join online activities that educate people about rain forest loss. For example, check out the Online Forest Photo Rally at http://www.environmental-action.org. You'll find many such activities on the websites listed at the end of this book.

• **Keep learning.** Visit rain forest websites often. Many sites add new information regularly. Visit the library for books about rain forests. Tell your friends and family what you've learned. Ask them to join you in protecting the world's rain forests.

GOING GREEN

HOW TO WRITE TO YOUR LEGISLATOR

Write your senator and representative. Ask them to support laws that help rain forests. Write key people in companies that do business in rain forests too.

You can send either letters or e-mails. Some environmental groups can provide form letters for you to sign. But a letter that you write yourself will carry more weight than a form letter. Here are tips for writing your legislator or the president of a company:

- **Say how you feel** about the rain forest. Use your own words. Explain how a certain law or business practice would affect you, your family and friends, your school, or your community. Use facts, not opinions, to make your case.

- **Keep your letter short.** Describe only one issue. If you're writing about a law, identify it by number and title if you can.

- **Ask for a reply.** This shows that rain forests are important to you.

- **Write a thank-you note** if your legislator or a businessperson helps rain forests in some way. That will help the person remember you next time you write.

- **Find postal and e-mail addresses** for U.S. legislators at http://www .senate.gov and http://www.house.gov. To contact a company, visit its website and click on the Contact Us link.

ENVIRONMENTAL GROUPS

Many environmental groups can help you learn more about rain forests and suggest ways to protect them. Here are just a few:

- **Conservation International**
  http://www.conservation.org
  2011 Crystal Drive, Suite 500
  Arlington, VA 22202
  703-341-2400 or 800-429-5660

- **The Nature Conservancy**
  http://www.nature.org
  4245 North Fairfax Drive, Suite 100
  Arlington, VA 22203-1606
  703-841-5300

- **Rainforest Action Network**
  http://ran.org
  221 Pine Street, 5th Floor
  San Francisco, CA 94104
  415-398-4404

- **World Wildlife Fund**
  http://www.worldwildlife.org
  1250 24th Street Northwest
  P.O. Box 97180
  Washington, DC 20090-7180
  202-293-4800

GLOSSARY

atmosphere: the layer of gases that surrounds Earth

basin: a broad area of land drained by a river

biodiverse: home to many different types of living things

bromeliad: one of a family of tropical and subtropical plants from the Americas that includes the pineapple

canopy: the layer of a rain forest near the treetops, where most of the forest's plants and animals live

climate: usual weather patterns, or the typical weather in a specific region

decay: rot or break down

deforestation: loss of forests by cutting, burning, or otherwise destroying trees

ecoregions: areas that share similar land, climate, and living things

ecosystem: a community of living things that depend on one another and their shared environment

emergent layer: the highest level of a rain forest, where the tallest treetops are

endangered: at risk of losing all members of a species, or kind, of animals forever

endemic: unique to a certain part of the world

epiphyte: plant that lives on other plants. An epiphyte gets food and water from air and rain.

extinct: gone forever. If a species is extinct, it means that no more individuals of that species can be born.

global warming: the warming of Earth because of increased carbon dioxide and other heat-trapping gases in the atmosphere. The theory of global warming has been supported by most scientific study.

greenhouse gas: a name for carbon dioxide and other gases that hold the sun's heat near Earth. Greenhouse gases cause global warming.

habitat: the type of place where a kind of plant or animal can live

indigenous: native

liana: vine

nutrient: a substance, such as a mineral, that helps living things survive and grow

poach: to hunt illegally

productive: when an ecosystem makes a lot of food for its members

species: a group of living things that shares certain characteristics and can mate and produce young

sustainable: practiced or used in a way that doesn't destroy or permanently damage a resource

understory: shady area between the rain forest canopy and the ground

SELECTED BIBLIOGRAPHY

Associated Press. "Top Scientists Warn of Water Shortages and Disease Linked to Global Warming." *New York Times*, March 12, 2007.

Boffey, Philip M. "The Evidence for Global Warming." *New York Times*, July 4, 2006.

Bradsher, Keith. "Push to Fix Ozone Layer and Slow Global Warming." *New York Times*, March 15, 2007.

Cowell, Alan. "Britain Drafts Laws to Slash Carbon Emissions." *New York Times*, March 14, 2007.

Duetsch, Claudia H. "Attention Shoppers: Carbon Offsets in Aisle 6." *New York Times* March 7, 2007.

Editorial. "A Green Deal on Coal." *New York Times*, February 28, 2007.

Editorial. "Reforestation and Deforestation." *New York Times*, November 20, 2006.

Hanley, Charles J. "The Future of the Amazon Is Key to the Earth's Fate, Scientists Say; Dieback Is Projected for the Massive Rain Forest, Leading to Release of Greenhouse Gas." *Los Angeles Times*, February 20, 2005.

Harder, Ben. "Two-Fifths of Amazonian Forest Is at Risk." *Science News*, April 8, 2006.

Harvey, HaiSong, ed. *Rain Forests*. Detroit: Greenhaven Press, 2002.

Higgins, Michella. "Carbon Neutral: Raising the Ante on Eco-Tourism." *New York Times*, December 10, 2006.

James, Ian. "Endangered Puerto Rican Parrots Get Chance at Survival." *Los Angeles Times*, April 3, 2005.

Lasky, Kathryn. *The Most Beautiful Roof in the World: Exploring the Rainforest Canopy*. Orlando, FL: Harcourt Brace and Company, 1997.

Lewington, Anna. *Atlas of Rain Forests*. Austin, TX: Raintree Steck-Vaughn, 1997.

Margolis, Mac. "Under Construction: Brazil Has Tried for Decades to Keep Developers Out of the Amazon." *Newsweek International*, April 11, 2005.

Marshall. *Rain Forests of the World*. New York: Marshall Cavendish, 2002.

New York Times. "Brazil to Protect Stretch of Amazon Rain Forest." Late East Coast edition, December 5, 2006.

Osnos, Evan. "Climate Shift Threatens a Way of Life; Rising Waters Caused by Global Warming Are Swamping Coastal Villages." *Los Angeles Times*, August 27, 2006.

Revkin, Andrew C. "Global Warming Trend Continues in 2006, Climate Agencies Say." *New York Times*, December 15, 2006.

Senior, Kathryn. *Rainforest*. London: Franklin Watts, 1999.

Smithsonian. "There Goes the 'Hood." January 2006.

USA Today Magazine. "Dry Season Produces Biggest Growth Spurt." June 2006.

Vegetarian Times. "Slash and Burn." October 2005.

Walk, Matthew L. "In a Test of Capturing Carbon Dioxide, Perhaps a Way to Temper Global Warming." *New York Times*, March 15, 2007.

Weekly Reader. "Animals of the Rain Forest." April 7, 2006.

———. "Paradise Lost? The Amazon Rain Forest Is Disappearing at an Alarming Rate." April 7, 2006.

Williams, Alex. "Have Guitar, Will Recycle." *New York Times*, March 15, 2007.

FURTHER READING

Blue Planet Biomes: Tropical Rainforest
   http://www.blueplanetbiomes.org/rainforest.htm
   This website provides information about the plants, animals, and climate of tropical rain forests, with a section offering additional information about rain forests in Southeast Asia.

Conservation International

http://www.conservation.org

This website offers tons of information about rain forest areas and how you can help them. Learn about different regions of the world, calculate how much carbon dioxide you add to the air, or read news updates.

Enchanted Learning: All about Rainforests

http://www.enchantedlearning.com/subjects/rainforest

This user-supported website includes short facts about rain forest structure and species. It also offers puzzles, quizzes, math activities, and an illustrated glossary.

Environmental Action

http://www.environmental-action.org

This organization began in the early 1970s and organized the first Earth Day in 1970. Its website offers information, news updates, and calls to action on global warming, wilderness, air pollution, energy independence, and other environmental topics.

Kelsey, Elin. *Strange New Species: Astonishing Discoveries of Life on Earth*. Toronto: Maple Tree Press, 2005. This book combines great pictures with action-packed adventure stories. Meet scientists who travel the world seeking new species. Learn about strange new life-forms they're discovering in rain forests and other places.

Learning about Rainforests

http://www.srl.caltech.edu/personnel/krubal

This website describes rain forests and where they grow. It provides information on the plants, animals, and people of the rain forest. It also describes how people are destroying rain forests and what we can do to stop deforestation.

Lewington, Anna. *Atlas of Rain Forests*. Austin, TX: Raintree Steck-Vaughn, 1997. This large book contains lots of color pictures and maps. It describes the value of rain forests and why we need to protect them.

Mongabay.com
> http://rainforests.mongabay.com
> One person created this site based on what he learned traveling in rain forest areas. A special kids' section offers information about rain forests and the animals and plants living in them. The adult section is packed with information, charts, and news updates.

Natural Resources Defense Council
> http://www.nrdc.org
> This organization works to "save wild places." Its website gives information about global warming, oil, air, water, wildlife, health, and laws. It also offers ideas on helpful actions individuals can take.

The Nature Conservancy
> http://www.nature.org
> Stories and pictures abound on this website. You can join its online activities to receive free e-newsletters. Members also can build their own nature pages.

Pratt-Serafini, Kristin Joy. *A Walk in the Rainforest.* Nevada City, CA: Dawn Publications, 2007.   This book offers an alphabetical tour of the rain forest. Each page includes a picture and description of a different plant or animal.

Wet Tropics Management Authority
> http://www.wettropics.gov.au
> This website provides information about the environment and people of the Wet Tropics World Heritage Area in Australia. It offers plentiful resources for teachers and students, research information, a media section, and much more.

World Wildlife Fund
> http://www.worldwildlife.org
> Learn about endangered species and rain forests worldwide at this jam-packed website. In the "fun and games" section, you can take a tiger quiz, send e-mails to friends, and play games.

69

INDEX

ABOUT THE AUTHOR

Anne Welsbacher has written about wading birds, pelicans, and the Hawaiian rain forest for Lerner Publications as well as other books on animals, physical sciences, and the states. She has lived in Minnesota, California, and Kansas. She enjoys the animals and plants that live in all those states—especially in the tall grasses of Kansas.

PHOTO ACKNOWLEDGMENTS

The images in this book are used with the permission of: © John Kreul/Independent Picture Service, p. 1 (background); © Royalty-Free/CORBIS, pp. 1 (type), 3 (background); © iStockphoto.com/Mark Kostich, p. 1 (left); © iStockphoto.com/George Manga (palm tree); © Kitchen & Hurst /leesonphoto/drr.net, p. 3 (top); © iStockphoto.com/ranplett, p. 3 (bottom); © James Gritz/Robert Harding World Imagery/Getty Images, p. 4 (left inset); © Fotolia.com - headshot, p. 4 (right inset); NASA, pp. 4–5 (main); © Michael Fay/National Geographic/Getty Images, p. 5; Daniel Heuclin/NHPA/Photoshot, p. 6; © Warren E. Faidley/DRK PHOTO, p. 7; © Lynn M. Stone/DRK PHOTO, p. 9 (main); © Ed George/National Geographic/Getty Images, p. 9 (inset); © Bill Hauser/Independent Picture Service, pp. 10, 12; © Fotolia.com - Robyn Mackenzie, p. 11; © Nancy Nehring/Photodisc/Getty Images, p. 13; © Michael Fogden/DRK PHOTO, pp. 14 (top), 25 (inset), 30; © iStockphoto.com/Adam Kazmierski, p. 14 (bottom); © Elena Elisseeva/Dreamstime.com, p. 15; © Martin Harvey/DRK PHOTO, pp. 17, 20, 35 (inset), 36, 38, 49 (main); © Jacques Jangoux/drr.net, p. 18; © NASA via Getty Images, p. 22; © M-Sat Ltd/Photo Researchers, Inc., p. 25 (main); © iStockphoto.com/Karel Broz , p. 26; © Pete Oxford/naturepl.com, p. 27; © David Cavagnaro/DRK PHOTO, p. 28; © Michael Thompson/Dreamstime.com, p. 29; © Pete Oxford/DRK PHOTO, p. 31; © Tom & Pat Leeson/DRK PHOTO, p. 32; © All Canada Photos/Alamy, p. 33; © Planetary Visions Ltd./Photo Researchers, Inc., pp. 35 (main), 39; AP Photo/Schalk van Zuydam, p. 37; © Arup Shah/DRK PHOTO, p. 40; AP Photo/Geoff Spencer, p. 41; © Justin Guariglia/National Geographic/Getty Images, p. 42; © Ken Lucas/Visuals Unlimited, p. 43 (left); © Nick Garbutt/naturepl.com, p. 43 (right); © Maria Stenzel/National Geographic/Getty Images, p. 44; © Belinda Wright/DRK PHOTO, p. 45; © Michele Westmorland/drr.net, p. 46; © iStockphoto.com/pomortzeff, p. 47; © Tim Sloan/AFP/Getty Images, p. 49 (inset); © Andy Nelson/Christian Science Monitor/Getty Images, p. 50 (main); © Theo Allofs/Visuals Unlimited, p. 50 (inset); AP Photo/Pedro Ugarte/Pool, p. 53; AP Photo/Achmad Ibrahim, p. 55; © Tony Karumba/AFP/Getty Images, p. 57; © Paul Morigi/WireImage/Getty Images, p. 58; AP Photo/Aaron Harris, p. 59; © Jonathan A. Meyers/Photo Researchers, Inc., p. 61.

Cover: © John Kreul/Independent Picture Service (waterfall); © Royalty-Free/CORBIS (trees, type and spine background); © Sue Cunningham Photographic/Alamy (red plant); © iStockphoto.com/ranplett (toucan); © iStockphoto.com/Mark Kostich (frog); © iStockphoto.com/George Manga (palm tree).